GRACIE AND THE GALAPANZAS

- -

A one-act drama for high school or college

by
John Glass

☛ ☛

www.studentplays.org
john@studentplays.org

<u>Copyright information. Please read!</u>

☞ About StudentPlays ☜

Student Plays consists of **John Glass, Jackie Jernigan,** and **Dominic Torres.** We are a group of playwrights and directors that have written scripts for elementary school through college. We are proud of the variety of ages that our scripts serve.

Student Plays has "creepy" plays, and we also have Latino-themed plays. These are scripts that focus on Latino youths and the Latino experience. Any school can perform a Latino-themed play: it just requires a general introduction and basic exposure to the Spanish language, something that most schools and students already have.

To learn more, visit www.studentplays.org, or to contact one of the playwrights directly, simply email us at john@studentplays.org.

☆ <u>Characters</u> ☆

GRACIE GALAPANZA 20s. Emotional, angry. Tightrope walker and trapeze artist.

FRANK 30s. Kind, caring. Security guard.

PALÓN 40s-60s. A famous tightrope walker.

POLICE OFFICER # 1 Extremely brief role, at the end of the play. Any gender.

POLICE OFFICER # 2 Extremely brief role, at the end of the play. Any gender.

The time is 1980, and the setting is two small rooms in New York's Twin Towers. The rooms are in different towers, and they directly face each other through <u>two windows</u>.

One room is stage left, the other stage right. 95 percent of the play takes place in GRACIE's room.

Each room is a simple setup of one chair and a small table. There is a telephone is GRACIE's room, and also a small balancing pole. The two windows can be a simple arrangement. They could be made from cardboard, or thin pieces of wood or light aluminum tubing, something that could easily be taken on and off the stage.

Throughout the play, GRACIE holds a handgun, which she waves menacingly as she holds FRANK hostage. She must wield the gun throughout the play so as to maintain control and power over FRANK. GRACIE is wearing a bandana or tights or clothing that resembles a professional tightrope walker.

Broken glass can be scattered in front of GRACIE's window, as GRACIE has smashed the window in order to construct the tightrope. A bow/crossbow and small bags stuffed with steel tools are also lying about her room. If desired, a simple tightrope can be devised between the rooms to reinforce a good visual of the setting.

SCENE ONE

At RISE: *GRACIE is pacing the room, holding a handgun. FRANK is seated, staring out the open window. The lights are down on the other room.*

GRACIE I still can't believe this. You've never heard of the Flying Galapanzas?? Man!

FRANK I told you. I don't really follow such things.

GRACIE And you've lived in New York all your life?

FRANK Yes.

GRACIE Me and my brothers toured all over! Baltimore. Jersey City. Syracuse. I was the youngest person to ever walk the Blue Towers in Philadelphia!

FRANK No kidding?

GRACIE Yes, yes. Unbelievable. Frank, I thought you were hipper than that.

FRANK I remember that my wife used to read about Palón. But that was years ago.

GRACIE Well, of course! *Everybody* followed Palón! I should be so lucky!

FRANK Well, not *everybody.*

GRACIE Whatever. He needs to get here soon.

FRANK You heard me on the phone! They're trying to locate him.

GRACIE He needs to hurry up. He's gonna watch me walk this wire!

FRANK He will. He will . . .

GRACIE Staten Island's not *that* far, and I know that's where Palón lives. They better not be trying any funny business!

FRANK He'll be here. I promise.

GRACIE Hmmph. Okay.

　　(Pause.)

FRANK Um. Gracie?

GRACIE What?

FRANK I beg your pardon, but—

GRACIE Why do people say that?

FRANK I . . . beg your pardon?

GRACIE See, there you go again. How do you 'beg someone's pardon'?

FRANK Uh, I don't know. It's just a, you know, a—

GRACIE Talk, friend. What do you want to say?

FRANK What's the purpose of all this? I've been sitting here listening to you talk for almost an hour. You toured all over! You did it *all*, you said. At such a young age!

GRACIE Well, sort of.

FRANK Sort of?

GRACIE I *did* tour all over, yes. We did the Niagara Falls. The Albany State Bridge. Lots of things. Shoot, the Flying Galapanzas once made the cover of the New York Post. And I was still in high school then!
    (Pause.)
But things just . . .

FRANK Things just *what?*

GRACIE Just never mind! Don't ask so many questions!

FRANK Sorry.

GRACIE And you better be sure that *only Palón* is in that room! *(Pointing out the window.)* Room 9032! Right where I can see him! Him and nobody else!

FRANK You heard me tell the police! They know!

GRACIE Don't you forget who's in control here.
    (Waves the gun.)

FRANK Okay. I'm not.

GRACIE Good.

>   *(Pause. GRACIE sighs, tries to relax. FRANK is looking out the window.)*

GRACIE So . . . you, uh, see her yet?

FRANK Um. No. Not yet.

GRACIE Which floor is it?

FRANK 88. Two floors down.

GRACIE Oh. Yeah.

FRANK *(Pointing outside.)* Right there on the corner. That last office. *(Pause.)* I usually work downstairs in the lobby. But sometimes I come up, you know, to some of the higher floors, and I try to see her while she's working. You know, when we're not too busy.

GRACIE What does she do?

FRANK She's a secretary for Bonanza Comics.

GRACIE Shut up! Bonanza Comics?

FRANK Yep. For 7 years.

GRACIE No way. Does she work with all the big writers? The Incredible Hulk? The Flash?

FRANK No, no. That's DC and Marvel.

GRACIE Oh.

FRANK Bonanza is a smaller company. She's just a secretary, you know.

GRACIE Wow. I love comic books. Aquaman. Batman. I really like the Flash. *(Beat.)* You're not kidding around, are you? Is that really what you've been looking at? Trying to find your wife?

FRANK Yes! I've actually been coming up to this floor almost every day this week.

GRACIE Why *this* week?

FRANK Oh, no reason, really.

GRACIE Why this week?

FRANK It's an important week.

GRACIE Important?

FRANK Yes. That's all.

GRACIE What are you talking about?

FRANK Nothing. It's just an important time for us.

GRACIE *(Waving the gun.)* Frank . . .?

FRANK Yes?

GRACIE I'm tired, Frank. And I like direct communication. Now tell me: what the hell is so important about *this* week?

FRANK Our daughter died exactly three years ago. *That's* what.

GRACIE What? You have *kids?* You're so young!

FRANK Well. I *had* a kid.

GRACIE Oh. Okay. Sorry.

FRANK That's okay. She died on August 6, 1977. It'll be three years on Thursday.

GRACIE Wow. Um. How?

FRANK Hmm?

GRACIE How did she die?

FRANK Um. My daughter?

GRACIE Yes.

FRANK She died in a car crash. On Belt Parkway. In Brooklyn.

GRACIE Oh. Yeah. Belt Parkway can be rough.

FRANK Yeah. So, you know. There's been a lot of depression in the house right now. This time of year there's always a lot of depression.

GRACIE Well. Man. That's too bad.

FRANK And so, you know, I come up here. It's beautiful this time of day. The sun is so golden as it hits the glass of all those buildings. It's almost mesmerizing. I come up here and try to see my wife.
    (Long pause as he fumbles for the words.)
 And at the same time, I try to forgive myself for letting it happen.

GRACIE Have you ever seen her?

FRANK My wife? Amazingly, no. I never have. The South Tower is only a few hundred feet across. But there are a lot of people walking around, you know. So it's hard to tell. I know exactly where her office is. But I have yet to see her.

GRACIE Wow. Hmm. In the same building as the Flash, huh?

FRANK No, I told you, that's—

GRACIE Do you think the Flash could walk a tightrope as well as I can?

FRANK The Flash? Uh, well, I don't know.

GRACIE The answer is *no*!

FRANK Okay.

GRACIE Nobody can match the talents of the great highwire artist Gracie Galapanza!!

> *(She mimes walking across a highwire, then stares out the window.)*

FRANK Okay. Not even the Flash?

GRACIE Nope! Not even the Flash! *(Beat. Points the gun at him.)* Well, there is actually *one* person. And that one person had better get here soon. Let's get on the phone again, Mr. Frank. I need to remind these people that time is running out.

FRANK *(Picking up the receiver, begins to dial.)* Okay.

GRACIE I've got a wire to walk!

(Lights fade to black. End of scene.)

SCENE TWO

At RISE: *As the lights go up, we see GRACIE and PALÓN both on the telephone, facing each other through the windows. As the towers are about 200 feet apart, the two cannot <u>clearly</u> see each other. GRACIE is still holding the gun, and FRANK is still sitting, though he fidgets from time to time. Three hours have passed.*

GRACIE Well, finally. I don't believe what I'm looking at. The one and the only . . . Palón.

PALÓN How are you?

GRACIE That is you, isn't you? *(Shields her eyes as she squints through the window)* It had better be you.

PALÓN Relax. It's me. I see you. You're Gracie Galapanza, right?

GRACIE That's right. You've . . . you've heard of me?

PALÓN I actually have.

GRACIE Yeah, whatever. It took them almost two hours to track you down so I'm sure that they told you all about me. I'm sure they—

PALÓN Stop. I know who you are. The Flying Galapanzas, right?

GRACIE Yes.

PALÓN I haven't seen you in person. But I know about you guys. You and your brothers, right? You guys did circuses, I believe?

GRACIE Well, yeah. Circuses, primarily. But we also did the Albany State Bridge. And Atlantic City.

PALÓN Right. You were a teenager then.

GRACIE Yep. And of course I had my solo career *(Pause.)* Nothing like yours, of course.

PALÓN Well, what I had was a long time ago.

GRACIE But you were the greatest.

PALÓN Well. I had my day. I'm not sure that I—

GRACIE And today I'm going to match what you did.

PALÓN I—I beg your pardon?

GRACIE *(Motioning to both FRANK and PALÓN)* Damn. You two aren't related, are you?

PALÓN Huh? What??

GRACIE Nothing. Nothing. *(Beat.)* Yep. Today I will match the legendary Palón, and prove that I too am one of the greatest!

PALÓN Gracie, come on. It's two-hundred feet from tower to tower! And it's a very windy day.

GRACIE The wind will die down soon enough! And anyway, it was windy when *you* did it, in 1974. In these same two towers! Ninety stories up! And how many times did *you* go back and forth? Huh?

PALÓN Well . . .

GRACIE How many??

PALÓN Eight.

GRACIE Ahh! Eight times! On a tightrope!! Amazing! *(Beat as she sees FRANK moving around.)* What are you doing, Frank??

FRANK Um. Nothing.

GRACIE How about sitting still for me? I'd hate to have to use this gun.

FRANK Sorry! My legs are stiff. But Gracie, it *is* windy out there!! It's gotten worse!

PALÓN Gracie, look—

GRACIE Shut up! Both of you! You're going to watch me walk this!! And that's all there is to it! *(Checking the wind out the window)* The wind should be dying down very soon.

PALÓN I know about your family's big fall, Gracie. And I'm sorry.

GRACIE The cops told you about that too, huh?

PALÓN I really am sorry. But is it worth all of this? A hostage situation? Why don't you let me help you?

GRACIE I wasn't affected by that fall.

PALÓN But your brothers *were*. And . . . are you sure that *you* weren't affected by it as well?

GRACIE Lay off. We used faulty gear. I'm over it.

PALÓN I know what happened, Gracie. I know that you blame yourself for the accident. I've . . . I've been there.

GRACIE You know *everything*, don't you? Think you're real smart, huh? Is there anything those idiot cops *didn't* tell you? I bet they can't wait to grab me the minute I cross over to the South Tower! Snatch me up, throw me in jail!

PALÓN It's just not safe. The wind is really strong today. It's crazy out there.

GRACIE I told you, it will die down. It did for your performance.

PALÓN Well . . .

GRACIE It will.

> *(Beat.)*

PALÓN Um. So what kind of cable do you have out there?

GRACIE 257. Triple-knotted.

PALÓN Mmmm.

GRACIE Don't worry. This time I made sure it was done right.

PALÓN Did you use a bow and arrow to get the cable across? To this side?

GRACIE Yep. Same as you. Hell, I used your whole playbook.

PALÓN Ha. Well, I'm gratified.

GRACIE It took all night but we pulled it off. Me and my crew used fake security badges.

PALÓN: Mh-hmmm.

GRACIE: Had access to the freight elevator. Paid off some security guards. Bunch of suckers. Well . . . *(Looking at FRANK.)* All but *one*, that is. At least, I can tolerate Frank. Isn't that right, man?

(FRANK laughs slightly.)

GRACIE Yep. I can tolerate Frank.

(Loud static is heard as the phones begin to gradually conk out.)

GRACIE Hello? *(More static.)* Hey!! PALÓN? HELLO?

(She taps phone several times. PALÓN also tries to make his phone work to no avail. He then exits quietly, carrying the phone with him. Lights go down on him.)

GRACIE HELLO? What happened?

FRANK The phones up here do that sometimes, Gracie.

GRACIE Hello?? *(Hangs up angrily, glares out the window.)* DAMMIT!! They better not be trying any tricks!! He's gonna watch me do this!!

(Pause as she checks the wind again, and collects herself.)

GRACIE Stupid telephone. Stupid wind.

FRANK Gracie?

GRACIE WHAT?

FRANK You're *not* an old lady. You're not even thirty years old. You could go to college! Or resurrect your career!

GRACIE Oh, stop. I tried, Frank. I tried everything.

FRANK Maybe you didn't try hard enough. Maybe—

GRACIE Shut up and get over here.

FRANK I beg your—oh, uh, *what?*

GRACIE Come over here!

(FRANK makes his way to the window.)

GRACIE Look at this. It's about that time of day, isn't it? *(Pause as they stare at the sunlight.)* Look at that sunlight. I gotta hand it to you, Frank. You were right. It really is a sight to see.

FRANK Yes, it is.

GRACIE Which floor is she on?

FRANK Oh, um, my wife's floor? 88th. Her office is right on the corner. See it? The one with the green trim right above it.

GRACIE I see it. Cool. That's where Aquaman and the Flash hang out, huh?

FRANK Well. In a manner of speaking, yes.

(Pause. They stare at the tower.)

GRACIE So. I know about your wife. But then there's your daughter. Being up here reminds you of her, you said? Whenever you see this?

FRANK I think about my daughter all of the time. But yeah . . . especially when I come up here, this time of day. When I see those—wow, just look at that—those wonderful golden lasers shooting against all that glass and steel.

GRACIE I know. So gorgeous.

FRANK Right here in the greatest city on the planet. Yeah, I think about how I should have been there for her.
        (Pause.)
And when I look at this, it's like I'm seeing a piece of her. You know? Her face, so young. Somewhere within all of that golden light I can actually see her. I can actually see them *both*.

(Long pause as they stare.)

GRACIE Frank?

FRANK Yeah?

GRACIE Do you . . . really think that I could outperform the Flash? On that highwire?

FRANK I think you could do a lot of things, Gracie. You're a pro. You could do something like this walk without so much drama.

GRACIE But it's too late, Frank.

FRANK What's too late?

GRACIE I tried everything. I tried to make a comeback. Nobody cares!

FRANK Yes they do.

> *(Enter PALÓN in his room, holding a new phone. He quickly enters, dialing.)*

GRACIE There are some things in life you just can't get past. And anyway, do you know how many people came to my solo show last year in Long Island? Twenty-five. Twenty-five people! My name is no good anymore! People blame *me* for what happened!

FRANK *I* care.

GRACIE What?

FRANK I hardly know you. But Gracie . . . *I* care.

(*The telephone rings. She picks up, and FRANK sits down. A light goes up on PALÓN.*)

GRACIE Yeah? Palón? Is that you?

PALÓN I think we've got the phones working again.

GRACIE Okay, good.

PALÓN Listen, Gracie, I—

GRACIE No more talking, my friend. I am *doing* this. This is it! The wind should be dying down. (*Sticks her head out, checks the wind.*) Not that the wind ever stopped you.

PALÓN But Gracie, the wind *should* have stopped me.

GRACIE What are you talking about?

PALÓN I lost an apprentice to strong winds. At the Notre Dame, in Paris.

GRACIE At your big walk in 1975? I saw that on television! No you didn't!

PALÓN Yes I did! Hardly anybody knows. But it's true. During practice runs that same week my apprentice fell. I got in a hurry.

GRACIE Hmm. Wow.

PALÓN You know, trying to rush everything. Why do you think I haven't done a big-time walk like that since then?

(Pause.)

GRACIE Well. I've sort of always wondered why.

PALÓN You aren't the only person to ever lose someone. Or to feel guilty. Good God, girl, you could still do a lot! You haven't conquered enough things to be this depressed!!

GRACIE Excuse me?

PALÓN You haven't! You haven't walked the Eiffel Tower, have you?

GRACIE The Eiffel Tower?

PALÓN Yes! What about Kings Island, in Ohio? Or the Grand Canyon? You aren't the only one to—

(Loud static. The phone connection is once again cut off.)

GRACIE Hello?? Palón? Not again!!

PALÓN Gracie? Gracie??

> *(They both furiously try to make the phones work. Lights go down on PALÓN as he eventually exits quietly, carrying the phone, frustrated.)*

GRACIE PALÓN? HELLO?? NO! *(Slams phone down, looks across at the window.)* Whatever! No more waiting! He's gonna watch me do this right now!! *(She grabs the pole, prepares to climb out.)*

FRANK Gracie??

GRACIE No more blabbering! This is it!!

FRANK What *about* the Eiffel Tower, Gracie?

GRACIE What the hell are you saying?

FRANK Isn't that what you guys were just talking about? How you haven't walked it yet?

GRACIE No!

FRANK *(Gradually becoming more emotional.)* See?? There *are* plenty of places where you can perform. Bigger, high-profile walks!!

GRACIE Shuddup!

FRANK You aren't ready for *this* one! Not today!

GRACIE I'm done trying, Frank, I told you.

FRANK You are rushing all of this!!

GRACIE No, I'm not!!

FRANK You could actually walk these two towers one day! Properly and legally, and—

GRACIE Stop!

FRANK Gracie, think about Palón! I could almost hear him talking to you just then! He's had his share of misery, hasn't he? God knows I've had mine!

GRACIE Frank, stop it!

FRANK I can't deal with SOMEBODY ELSE DYING!! I JUST CAN'T!! *(He begins to break down.)* I can't deal with another death . . .

> *(Long pause as he sobs. GRACIE collects her breath.)*

GRACIE Look, Frank . . . car crashes happen. Even if you *had* been there, your daughter would have probably died. Right? And nobody's going to die here.

FRANK It's still windy out there! It's dangerous! You aren't prepared for this and you know it! Gracie, you have too much to live for to chance this!!
    (Pause.)
And dammit . . . I know we don't even know each other. But I—I don't want to lose somebody else! I can't *handle* losing *one* more person. I've already been through too much!!
    (Pause.)
I *do* care, Gracie. Isn't that enough?? Isn't the concern of one human being enough??

    (Another long pause. FRANK sobs lightly.)

GRACIE You . . . really mean all of that?

FRANK You bet I do. Every damn word of it.

GRACIE Well . . . it's awful kind of you, Frank. It is. But . . . *(Beat. She moves to the window again.)* But, no. I'm doing this. Right now.

FRANK GRACIE!!

GRACIE I'm doing this, Frank.

FRANK Gracie, NO!!

GRACIE Shut up, Frank!

FRANK You can't go out there!! *(He tackles her from behind.)*

GRACIE HEY!!

FRANK You just can't go out there!!

> *(Enter the two police officers, quickly. They rush over and restrain GRACIE.)*

FRANK It's too risky, Gracie!!

GRACIE Get away! GET YOUR HANDS OFF ME!!

POLICE OFFICER # 1 Grab her!

FRANK It's going to be all right, Gracie.

POLICE OFFICER # 2 Got her.

GRACIE Let me go, you bastards!!

FRANK Gracie!! Calm down!

GRACIE No!!

FRANK It's going to be okay.

GRACIE Let me go! Ohhh . . *(Begins to cry.)*

POLICE OFFICER # 1 It's okay, miss.

FRANK It's going to be all right, Gracie. It's going to be all right.

> *(He repeats this as GRACIE sobs loudly. They hold her tightly, and he continues to console her. Lights fade. End of scene.)*

SCENE THREE

At RISE: *Before the lights go up, we heard a telephone ringing. Then, only two small lights go up on the stage, one on GRACIE and the other on FRANK. They are on opposite sides of the stage, sitting, each holding a telephone. GRACIE is calling FRANK at his home. She is dressed in a prison shirt/jumpsuit. A prison guard stands nearby.*

FRANK Hello?

GRACIE So . . . how's your tightrope walking coming along?

   (Pause.)

FRANK Gracie?

GRACIE The one and the only.

FRANK Wow. Hi. How ya doing?

GRACIE Well, pretty good, I guess. You?

FRANK I'm okay. Doing pretty good. This is a surprise.

GRACIE I suppose I got my wish.

FRANK Your wish?

GRACIE Yeah. You know. The New York Times. Front page of the Wall Street Journal. I'm famous.

FRANK *(Laughing.)* Yes, you are famous. Be careful of what you wish for, I guess.

GRACIE Yep.

FRANK Um, how long are you in for?

GRACIE Well. Not too long.

FRANK Yeah?

GRACIE Yeah. They gave me two years. Minimum security. Enough time to let me clear my head.

FRANK Well . . . you'd be proud of me. My tightrope skills are coming along pretty good. I've actually been out in my little backyard, practicing a bit.

GRACIE You have?

FRANK Yep. Ever since that day. You inspired me!

GRACIE Ha. Frank and the highwire!!

FRANK Yep. Tied a rope to two old posts. I'm learning. Of course, the wife . . . well, she would be worried that I'm up too high.

GRACIE How high are you?

FRANK Oh, about three inches from the ground.

GRACIE *(Laughing.)* Three inches??

FRANK Yeah.

GRACIE That's classic!

FRANK Yep. Not exactly ninety stories up.

  (Pause.)

GRACIE Mmmm. Look . . . I've only got a few minutes to talk. I just wanted to thank you.

FRANK Well. I didn't really do anything.

GRACIE Yes you did, Frank. Really. I wasn't well up there, that day in the tower. I think that's pretty obvious. I'm not well now. It's a good thing that you tackled me, and stopped me.
  (Pause.)
But I *know* I'm not well. And that's important. I'm getting some help while I'm in here. I'll get back to where I used to be.

(Pause.)
One day.

FRANK That's good to hear, Gracie. That really is *(Pause.)* Um . . . Gracie?

GRACIE Yeah?

FRANK I saw her.

GRACIE You saw who?

FRANK My wife. I saw my wife. At work, in the South Tower.

GRACIE You did?

FRANK I saw her this week.

GRACIE Wow. Did . . . did you tell her?

FRANK No. No, I think it's just something I'll keep to myself. But yeah, there she was, walking around, near one of the windows.

GRACIE Man.

FRANK Wearing that pretty olive-colored dress . . .

GRACIE Wow.

FRANK It was the same dress she had on the day she and my daughter got in the car . . . and drove off. *(Pause.)* Yep.

GRACIE Damn. You saw her. Was it one of those Manhattan afternoons, Frank?

FRANK Oh, yeah. Yeah. The sun's light was just everywhere. Golden and . . . and just gorgeous. Wish you could have seen it. It was something.
       (Pause.)
Gracie, I don't know how to express this . . . but something happened to me that day up in the tower, with you. I can't explain it, but . . . you really rejuvenated me.

GRACIE You don't have to explain, Frank. I think I understand.

FRANK You've kind of given me another chance. That's all.

GRACIE Yeah. I think I understand.

FRANK And for that . . . I thank you.

       (Pause.)

GRACIE I'll see you on the other side, Frank. You *and* the Flash.

FRANK Ha. Me *and* the Flash?

GRACIE That's right. Both of you.

FRANK Okay. Take care of yourself, Gracie.

GRACIE Bye, Frank.

FRANK Good-bye.

(They hang up. Lights go down on GRACIE, remain up on FRANK. He sits for a moment, thinking, and then he slowly smiles. Lights fade to black. End of play.)

☞ More from Student Plays ☜

Othello's Just Another Fellow

Dramedy. **Grades 5-7.** 25-35 minutes. 8 actors: 4 males, 3 females, one teacher (or student portraying a teacher) 3 to 5 extras, if needed. ****A Latino-themed play****

A group of students are involved in a school production of *Othello*, but one of them is disturbed about the lack of diversity in the play. He takes certain steps to disrupt the play but in the end is encouraged by the others to try and make a difference in another, more constructive way. A lesson is learned, and the production is saved from disaster!

Pagasqueeny's Pantry

Comedy. **Middle/High School.** 15-20 minutes. 6 actors: 3 females, 2 males. One student (or a teacher) plays the comical role of the elderly Mr. Pagasqueeny.

Three friends sneak into Mr. Pagasqueeny's home to get something that one of them left behind. But in walks Pagasqueeny and they must hide in the pantry! In this comical play, a lesson is learned about honesty and trust, but it takes a heated discussion in the pantry and a subsequent attempt to escape to find this out!

Una Carta de Abuelo

Dramedy. **Middle/High School.** 35-45 minutes. 10 actors: 1 teacher, 5 females, 4 males. (With the option of 4-5 extra actors in two scenes.)   **A Latino-themed play****

Two cousins discover an old letter in their late grandfather's comic collection that they think leads to treasure! The cousins often butt heads, with one believing that he is more "Mexican," the other believing that some people make too much of a fuss about "being Mexican." Thus, they form their *own* groups in search of what Grandpa hid long ago. But what they find is actually worth more than merely silver or gold.

Barbecue at the Prom!

Dramedy. **Grades 5-8.** 25-35 minutes. 6 actors: 3 females, 3 males

It's a classic tale of guys versus girls! It's a prom committee, and everybody is supposed to work together but differences and opinions get in the way, causing the guys and girls to form their groups. For the end-of-the-year prom, one side wants pasta and lace, the other wants sports and barbecue! The two groups square off but eventually work together, demonstrating the importance of cooperation and compromise.

Going to Guatemala

Dramedy. **High School.** 50-60 minutes. 11 actors. 6 males, 5 females.   ****A Latino-themed play****

A Latino student is chosen at the last minute to join a humanitarian group from his school that is headed to Guatemala. But since his Spanish is weak, he faces ridicule and criticism from certain peers. Jealousy and anger trickle throughout the campus as the trip approaches, and the social buzz of the high school becomes even more hectic when the student's trip money is stolen on campus, jeopardizing his trip.

Stravinsky's Kitchen

Comedy. **High School/College.** 12-15 minutes. 3 actors: 3 males (or females).

Two friends secretly enter the home of an employer to obtain a forgotten object but the homeowner abruptly arrives home while they are there. As they hide in the kitchen's pantry and plot their getaway, the two talk and eventually argue, exposing the true colors of one of them. Upon their hasty exit a mistake is made, and one of them capitalizes on this mistake, resulting in his/her fortune.

Forty Whacks

Drama. Spooky. **High School/College.** 25-35 minutes. 3 actors: 2 females, 1 male.

A pair of siblings have inherited the Lizzie Borden Bed and Breakfast in New England. Although the business was run for decades in a quiet, respectable fashion, one of the siblings is over-ambitious, wanting to unearth an alleged piece of buried evidence within the house. This brings about a chilly uneasiness between brother and sister, and perhaps within the house itself.

John Calhoun and a Thief

Drama. **College.** 35-40 minutes. 3 actors: 2 females, 1 male.

Kicked out of a university PhD program, a bitter and dejected female lifts from the library archives original copies of John Calhoun's personal documents. Counseled and consoled by her roommates, her conscience slowly gets to her; but as she seeks entry to other universities her luck turns to worse, and the subsequent decisions she makes regarding the historic papers cause this one-act play to become darker, if not funnier.

Honoring the Hijacker

Drama. **College.** 12-15 minutes. 4 actors: 2 females, 2 males.

It's 1981, the ten-year anniversary of the famed hijacker D.B. Cooper. The play's four characters are attending a "D.B. Festival" and have stayed up very late, outlasting everybody else. The late night chit-chat goes from pranks and jokes to outright volatility, and suddenly this get-together becomes something that three of the four characters didn't bargain for.

It's a Super Day at Sammy's!

Comedy. **Middle or High School.** 35-40 minutes. 9 actors: 5 females, 4 males (4 possible adults).

Jodi has found a summer job at a travel agency. But her three younger siblings can't seem to live without her! They call her at the office incessantly, which interferes with the work. The standard telephone greeting "It's a super day at Sammy's!" becomes a repeated theme of this comedy, as Jodi struggles to reach a balance between her job and her nagging siblings

Three Tenners

Comedy/Drama. **Elementary through High School.** Three Ten-Minute Plays.

Three Creepy Plays

Drama. **Middle School through College.** Three short 'creepy' plays.

Hockey Masks in Hueytown

Drama. Spooky. **High School/College.** 20-25
minutes. 4 actors: 2 males, 2 females.

Driving home for Thanksgiving break, four college
students stop off in a small rural town to retrieve one
of the student's old family pictures. They reluctantly
enter the empty home of his deceased uncle, a former
producer for the Friday the 13th movies. Strange
objects are found during their search . . but when a
hockey mask surfaces, everything really goes
sideways.

The Witch Makes Five

Drama. Spooky. **High School.** 10 minutes. 4 actors: 2
males, 2 females.

After a bizarre group camping trip, a student is
checked into a youth mental facility . When she is
visited by the other members of the trip, memories of
the weekend trickle out . . . and horrific things begin to
happen.

Mrs. Calapooza and the Culebra

Dramedy. **Grades 5-8.** 10 minutes. 5 actors: 3 females, 2 males.

Fed up with their grouchy teacher's classroom ways, four students complain and bicker back and forth during a Spanish quiz. The situation grows worse when the friends discover that one of them has pulled the ultimate prank on the teacher.

Raiders of the Lost Rakasa

Dramedy. **Grades 5-8.** 10 minutes. 7 actors: 4 females, 3 males.

Seven young explorers arrive at a cave in a far-off land in search of the great "Rakasa." They find what they want . . . along with a few of the cave's unexpected surprises.

www.ingramcontent.com/pod-product-compliance
Lightning Source LLC
Chambersburg PA
CBHW060544030426
42337CB00021B/4419